ALL
ABOUT
DOGS

PUGS

By Tammy Gagne

Consultant: Charlotte Patterson
Ivanwold Pugs, Destin, Florida

Capstone
press

Mankato, Minnesota

Edge Books are published by Capstone Press,
151 Good Counsel Drive, P.O. Box 669, Mankato, Minnesota 56002.
www.capstonepress.com

Library of Congress Cataloging-in-Publication Data
Gagne, Tammy.
    Pugs / by Tammy Gagne.
    p. cm. — (Edge books. All about dogs)
    Includes bibliographical references and index.
    ISBN-13: 978-1-4296-2031-4 (hardcover)
    ISBN-10: 1-4296-2031-5 (hardcover)
    1. Pug — Juvenile literature. I. Title. II. Series.
SF429.P9G34 2009
636.76 — dc22   2008001755

Summary: Describes the history, physical features, temperament, and care of
    the pug breed.

Editorial Credits
Gillia Olson, editor; Veronica Bianchini, designer; Marcie Spence,
    photo researcher

Photo Credits
Alamy/Juniors Bildarchiv, 6, 19; The Print Collector, 11; Robert McGouey, 15;
    Vintage Images, 12
Capstone Press/Karon Dubke, cover, 1, 13, 17 (both), 21, 22, 23, 24, 25, 27, 28
Dreamstime/Hanhanpeggy, 5
Getty Images Inc./Ariel Skelley, 26; John Arsenault, 18
Shutterstock/Albert Campbell, 9; Daniel Hughes, 16; John Steel, 29
Waldemar Dabrowski/123RF, 14

Capstone Press thanks Martha Diedrich, dog trainer, for her assistance
    with this book.

1 2 3 4 5 6 13 12 11 10 09 08

Table of Contents

CHAPTER 1

THE SERIOUS CLOWN

With their flat faces and serious expressions, pugs don't look like the friendliest dogs. Yet it only takes moments to see why the pug is such a popular pet. The pug has a delightful personality.

Is a Pug Right For You?

Pugs are natural clowns. They make it their life's work to entertain their owners with cute behavior and funny tricks. If you are missing a sock, your pug is the most likely thief. Plus, it won't give up the sock without a lap or two around the dining room table.

In addition to being funny, pugs are very loyal and loving animals. They want to be with their owners as much as possible. Because of their small size, they make excellent lap dogs.

Pugs are known for their clownish behavior.

When choosing a puppy, look for a healthy, friendly dog.

EDGE FACT

Pugs have small litters. Breeders must often put people who want puppies on waiting lists.

Of course, every dog **breed** has its downside. Some pugs snore. Pugs also make poor pets for highly active owners. A pug's short legs may have a hard time keeping up with you on a run or fast walk.

The pug's size may be a setback for athletics, but it can be an advantage in another way. Smaller dog breeds usually live longer than larger ones. Pugs can live well into their teens.

Finding a Pug

When searching for a pug, look for a healthy and friendly pup. Healthy pugs have shiny coats and bright eyes. They should not cough or have runny noses.

The best way to find a pug puppy is through a breeder. To find a breeder, check with a local pug breed club. Breed clubs teach people about a breed of dog.

Pugs may also be found through animal shelters and breed rescue groups. These organizations match people looking for pugs with dogs in need of homes. Many of these dogs make wonderful pets.

breed — a certain kind of animal within an animal group

CHAPTER 2

PUG HISTORY

The pug is sometimes called the Chinese pug. Most people believe the breed began in China about 2,500 years ago. Back then, a small dog called the *lo-sze* (LOW-zoo) was popular.

The *lo-sze* had a short face and a short coat like today's pug. This ancient breed also shared another quality with modern-day pugs — wrinkles. The way the breed's wrinkles were arranged on its face reminded people of the Chinese symbol for the word "prince." As a result, this feature became known as a prince mark. The name fit well because these dogs were kept by royalty.

The Pug's European History

The *lo-sze* made its way to Europe when the Dutch began trading with China. Dutch sailors brought these small dogs back to the Netherlands. They became popular with Dutch royalty. By the 1600s, people began to call them pugs.

Pug dogs and other breeds from China were known as lion dogs. Today you can find Chinese lion dog statues that look like a mix of a dog and a lion.

The first recorded pugs in Europe belonged to William III of Holland. William and English Princess Mary became co-rulers of England in 1689. By that time, their pugs were just as prized by the people as the king and queen were.

Other royalty also favored pugs. England's Queen Victoria and Empress Josephine Bonaparte of France owned pugs.

William Hogarth made pugs famous in his paintings. We know black pugs go as far back as 1730 because he painted one in *House of Cards*. He also painted a portrait of himself with his beloved pug.

The pug first competed in dog shows in England in 1861. By that time, two main breeding lines had formed — Willoughby and Morrison. Willoughby dogs were darker and thinner. Morrison dogs were lighter and stockier, like today's pug.

EDGE FACT

In 1572, a pug named Pompey saved the life of his master, Prince William the Silent. One night, Pompey heard noises and barked a warning. The noises were enemy soldiers. The barking woke the prince, who fled to safety.

Pug History in the United States

Pugs were first brought to the United States in 1885. The breed instantly became popular. By the early 1900s, though, pug numbers had fallen sharply. New breeds had taken people's interest from pugs. Fortunately, a small number of people kept breeding pugs. The Pug Dog Club of America formed in 1931. The same year, the breed was accepted by the American Kennel Club (AKC).

Though less popular, pugs were still being bred in the 1920s.

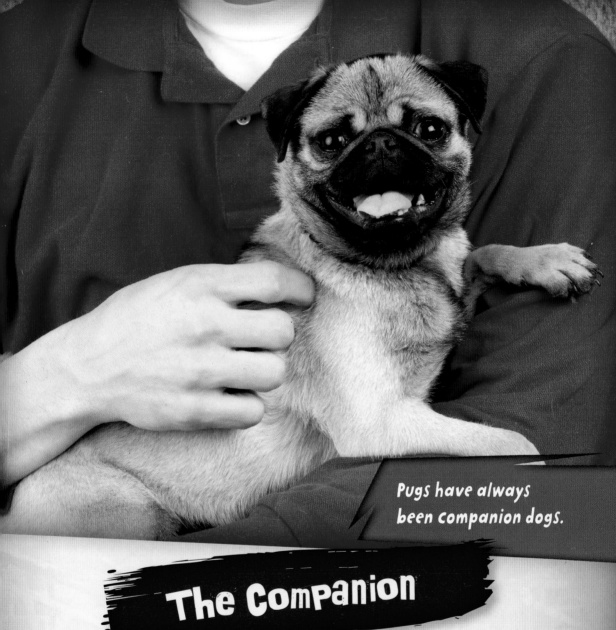

Pugs have always been companion dogs.

The Companion

While some dogs were bred for hunting or for herding, the pug was bred for companionship. These dogs have always enjoyed a warm lap and a loving owner. The pug's friendly personality makes it a favorite today. The pug is now in the top 30 breeds registered by the AKC.

CHAPTER 3

A STOCKY, WRINKLY BREED

The pug's name may have begun as a way to describe the breed. In the 1500s, a pug was a person who liked to tease or play tricks on people. The name "pug" may also have come from the Latin word *pugnus*, which means "fist." Viewed from the side, the breed's head looks like a closed fist.

Physical Features

The breed standard describes the way a pug should look. The pug's body is square and stocky. Adult pugs should weigh between 14 and 18 pounds (6 and 8 kilograms). Like its body, the pug's neck is thick. It supports a large, round head. Last, but not least, another famous pug feature is the curly tail. A tightly curled tail is preferred in dog shows.

breed standard — the physical features of a breed that judges look for in a dog show

The pug breed is known for its stocky body, wrinkled face, and curly tail.

The pug's face is perhaps its best-known feature. The wrinkles are large and deep. One full wrinkle over the pug's little nose is preferred. The dark eyes are very round and seem to stick out a bit. The small ears may be rose- or button-shaped. Button ears fold forward and fall flat. Rose ears fold more to the side and show some of the ear opening.

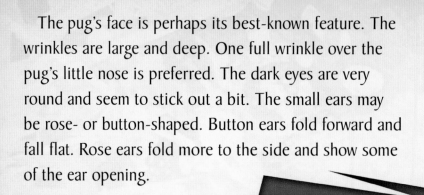

A pug should have one full wrinkle over its nose.

Pugs may be black or fawn.

The pug's coat is short and soft. The coat may be fawn or black. Fawn pugs have light yellow-gray fur. Their ears are black, and they have black shading on their faces called a mask. Fawn pugs also have black moles, or dots, on both cheeks and a black trace line down the center of its back.

EDGE FACT

The pug is the largest dog of the toy breeds. Toy breeds are the smallest purebred dogs.

Pugs are known for their friendliness. They quickly become part of the family.

Temperament

Pugs are known for having friendly **temperaments**. For this reason, the breed is a good choice for families with younger children. Of course, children should always be gentle with any dog. In the case of the pug, extra care must be taken not to hurt the dog's large eyes.

temperament — the way a dog usually acts or behaves

Some dogs bond most closely with just one family member, but most pugs love everyone — even strangers. They make quick friends with cats and other animals too. Owners do need to be sure large dogs won't hurt their pug.

Pugs delight in being the center of attention. They constantly entertain everyone around them with their clowning. Some even become jealous if people pay too much attention to another animal in the household.

Pugs tend to get along with other pets. They may even play together.

CHAPTER 4

CARING FOR A PUG

The pug may be a small dog, but owning one is a big responsibility. Pugs need care every day. Owners must train, feed, and groom their pugs. Pugs also need regular visits to a veterinarian.

Training a Pug

All dogs, even small breeds like the pug, need training. For puppies, learning usually begins with house-training. They need to learn to go to the bathroom outdoors or in a litter box. Dogs also need to be taught how to behave properly around people and other animals. Pugs can learn a variety of commands, such as "sit," "stay," and "come."

Training rewards can consist of words like "good dog," food treats, or a combination of the two. Always use a kind tone of voice when training your dog. Make training fun, and your pug will love learning new things.

Training your pug is an important part of its care.

Feeding a Pug

Few things have a greater effect on a dog's health than its diet. Eating a proper diet helps keep a dog looking and feeling its best.

Pugs may eat dry kibble or canned food. Some owners cook food especially for their pugs. What matters most is that the dog gets a balanced diet of the right vitamins, protein, and fat.

Foods made for growing puppies contain more calories and protein than adult foods. Pugs reach their adult size more quickly than larger dogs. But they still need the nutrients in puppy food until they are 1 year old.

A pug should always have plenty of fresh water. Drinking water allows nutrients to move throughout a dog's body. It also helps remove wastes from its system.

Pugs should always have plenty of fresh water.

Grooming a Pug

Pugs have double coats, which means they have two layers of fur. One is a soft undercoat. The other is a coarser topcoat. Because of all this hair, little pugs shed a surprising amount of fur. Owners should brush their dogs daily. Baths are only needed when a pug gets very dirty.

Certain parts of the pug need special attention. Trim its toenails and clean its ears about once a week. Ear cleanser can be purchased at pet supply stores.

Pugs need daily brushing. Their short coats hold a lot of fur!

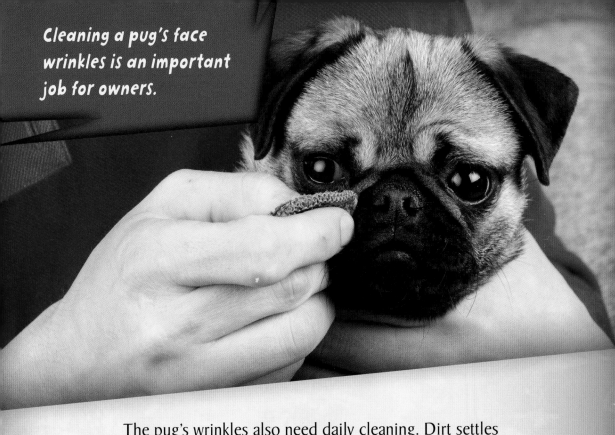

Cleaning a pug's face wrinkles is an important job for owners.

The pug's wrinkles also need daily cleaning. Dirt settles into these skin folds quickly. Use a wet cloth or baby wipe, but be sure to dry each wrinkle too.

Another daily task is brushing your pug's teeth. Because their mouths are often overcrowded, toy breeds are more likely to have tooth decay. Toothbrushes and toothpaste made for dogs are sold at most pet stores.

EDGE FACT

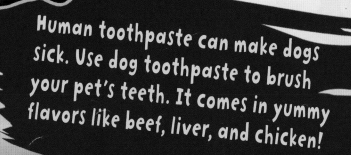

Human toothpaste can make dogs sick. Use dog toothpaste to brush your pet's teeth. It comes in yummy flavors like beef, liver, and chicken!

25

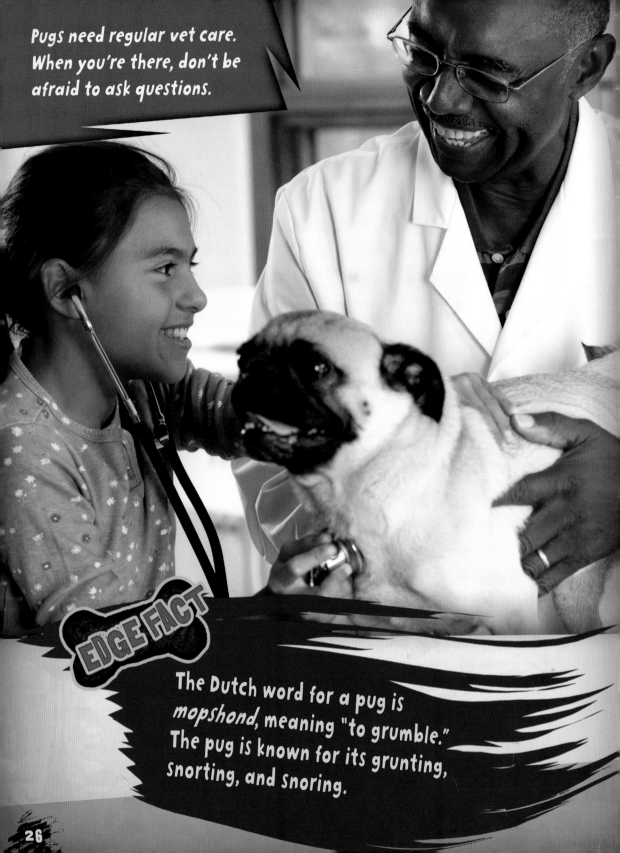

Pugs need regular vet care. When you're there, don't be afraid to ask questions.

EDGE FACT

The Dutch word for a pug is mopshond, meaning "to grumble." The pug is known for its grunting, snorting, and snoring.

Visiting the Vet

Another important part of dog care is a visit with the veterinarian at least once a year. Veterinarians are trained to treat sick or injured animals. A vet also helps healthy animals stay that way. At a yearly checkup, the vet will weigh your pug, take its temperature, and listen to its heart. The vet will also give your pet any needed **vaccinations**.

The veterinarian will ask you many questions during the visit. For example, how is house-training going? What are you feeding it? Is your pug getting enough exercise? You should also ask any questions that you have about your dog's care.

The vet will also check the pug's joints. Pugs sometimes suffer from hip dysplasia. The hip bones of a dog with dysplasia do not fit together properly. Pugs may also suffer from kneecap dislocation. The dog's kneecaps can pop out of place. Both joint conditions cause pain and make movement difficult.

vaccination — a shot of medicine that protects animals from disease

Keeping Your Pet Healthy

One of the best ways to keep a pug healthy is to have your vet spay or neuter it. These simple operations prevent a dog from ever having puppies. Fewer unwanted puppies helps control the pet population. It also reduces the animal's risk for many health problems, including cancer.

Pugs only need a small amount of exercise. Most can get their workouts from a short walk each day. These big-hearted little dogs will follow their owners from room to room all day long at home. Pugs don't make the best jogging partners, though. Their short noses make it difficult for them to breathe properly when they get hot.

The more you learn about caring for your pug, the better owner you will become. The rewards of caring for this little breed are anything but small. In return for your loving care, your pug will give you years of loyalty, laughs, and friendship.

A pug should have a short walk every day, perhaps past its favorite fire hydrant.

29

Glossary

breed (BREED) — a certain kind of animal within an animal group; breed also means to mate and raise a certain kind of dog.

breed standard (BREED STAN-durd) — the physical features of a breed that judges look for in a dog show

hip dysplasia (HIP diss-PLAY-zee-uh) — a condition in which an animal's hip bones do not fit together properly

neuter (NOO-ter) — a veterinary operation that prevents a male dog from producing offspring

protein (proh-TEEN) — a group of amino acids that helps body tissue grow and repair itself

spay (SPEY) — a veterinary operation that prevents a female dog from producing offspring

temperament (TEM-pur-uh-muhnt) — the combination of a dog's behavior and personality; the way an animal usually acts or responds to situations shows its temperament.

vaccination (vak-suh-NAY-shun) — a shot of medicine that protects animals from a disease

Read More

Borgeois, Dianne. *Pugs.* Animal Planet Pet Care Library. Neptune City, N.J.: T.F.H. Publications, 2006.

Gray, Susan H. *Pugs.* Domestic Dogs. Chanhassen, Minn.: Child's World, 2007.

Stone, Lynn M. *Pugs.* Eye to Eye with Dogs. Vero Beach, Fla.: Rourke, 2007.

Internet Sites

FactHound offers a safe, fun way to find Internet sites related to this book. All of the sites on FactHound have been researched by our staff.

Here's how:

1. Visit *www.facthound.com*
2. Choose your grade level.
3. Type in this book ID **1429620315** for age-appropriate sites. You may also browse subjects by clicking on letters, or by clicking on pictures and words.
4. Click on the **Fetch It** button.

FactHound will fetch the best sites for you!

Index